RESEARCH ON FINANCIAL BEHAVIORS AND USE OF SMALL-DOLLAR LOANS AND FINANCIAL SERVICES

LITERATURE REVIEW

Prepared for the US Department of the Treasury by the Urban Institute, 2010
Authors of this report are:

Brett Theodos, The Urban Institute

Jessica F. Compton, The Urban Institute

Abstract

This literature review provides an overview of research on the following small-dollar credit products: auto title loans, pawnshops, payday lending, refund anticipation loans (RALs) and checks (RACs), and rent-to-own (RTO). This review includes recently published research. It is not intended as an exhaustive treatment of these topics, but is designed to highlight key findings relevant for additional research.

Acknowledgments

This report was completed under contract to the U.S. Department of the Treasury under Order Number GS23F8198H/T09BPA017, with funds authorized by the U.S. Department of the Treasury.

Oversight and review were provided by the U.S. Department of the Treasury's Office of Financial Education and Financial Access. The report benefited from the experience and advice provided by Signe-Mary McKernan and Nancy Pindus.

The Urban Institute is a nonprofit, nonpartisan policy research and educational organization that examines the social, economic, and governance problems facing the nation. The views expressed are those of the authors and should not be attributed to the Urban Institute, its trustees, or its funders.

Small-Dollar Loan Products and Financial Services Definitions

Auto Title Loan

Auto title loans are small short-term loans secured by a borrower's vehicle. The loan amount is usually based on the car's worth. Additional charges, such as processing fees, may apply and a lump sum payment is usually due at the end of the loan term. The borrower generally keeps possession of the car during the term of the loan but leaves the title with the lender as security for repayment of the loan. The lender may require a copy of the keys to facilitate repossession in the event of default. If the borrower is unable to repay the loan at maturity, the lender frequently renews the loan while introducing additional charges. If the borrower continues to not pay, the lender may repossess the car. Also, rather than making the full payment at the end of the loan term, borrowers may pay the accrued interest and roll over the principal amount into a new loan which may also introduce additional fees to the consumer. Title lenders may also refer to their loans as "sales and leasebacks," "title pawns," or "motor vehicle equity lines of credit."[1] Auto title loans have a typical term of one month and loan sizes range between $600 and $2,500.[2] One survey found that 7 percent of the U.S. population reported using an auto title loan in the past five years (Applied Research and Consulting 2009).

Pawnshop Loan

The pawn process allows customers to pledge property as collateral and, in return, receive a small-dollar loan. Pawn loans are made on everything from jewelry to electronics. If the pawn customer chooses to redeem the loan, the collateral is returned upon repayment of the loan and the regulated fee. The option to redeem the collateral remains with the customer until the expiration of the contract. If the customer elects not to redeem his or her collateral by repaying the loan, there is no credit consequence to the borrower and the items are sold by the pawnbroker to retail consumers. Pawn transactions are the only type of consumer credit that requires reporting to local law enforcement agencies. In many states this reporting is required daily and must include personal information about the consumer (i.e., ethnicity, gender, address). Much of this information qualifies as nonpublic personal information under federal privacy law and is entitled to protection as such.[3] Additional reporting and research on pawnbrokers has noted the increasing numbers of pawn sales through the Internet on sites such as eBay (see Caskey 2005). The typical pawnshop loan lasts for one month and is worth less than $100.[4] According to a report by Applied Research and Consulting (2009), 8 percent of people in the U.S. report using a pawn loan in the past five years.

Payday Loan

A payday loan is a small unsecured, short-term loan that is usually repaid on the borrower's next payday. Customers are required to supply a few supporting documents, including proof of a regular income, a personal checking account, and identification. When the customer is approved for the payday loan, he or she writes a personal check for the amount of the advance plus a fee. The lender advances

---

[1] Amanda Quester and Jean Ann Fox, 2005, *Car Title Lending: Driving Borrowers to Financial Ruin*, Washington DC: The Center for Responsible Lending and The Consumer Federation of America.

[2] South Carolina Appleseed Legal Justice Center, 2004, *Auto Title Loans and the Law*, Columbia: South Carolina Appleseed Legal Justice Center.

[3] National Pawnbrokers Association, http://www.nationalpawnbrokers.org.

[4] National Pawnbrokers Association, 2008, *Pawnbroking Industry Overview: Meeting the Needs of America's Working Families*, Keller, TX: National Pawnbrokers Association.

the customer funds immediately but holds the check until an agreed -pon date, usually within two to four weeks, when the borrower receives his or her next paycheck. Payday loans average $250–$350, typically for two weeks. For a $100 loan, fees average $15—$20 (Flannery and Samolyk 2005). Using data from a nationally representative survey, Applied Research and Consulting (2009) found that 5 percent of respondents reported using a payday loan in the past five years.

Refund Anticipation Loan (RAL) or Check (RAC)

A refund anticipation loan (RAL) is money borrowed by a taxpayer from a lender based on the taxpayer's anticipated income tax refund. RALs are interest-bearing loans that allow a taxpayer to receive his or her refund from a lender before receiving it from the IRS. With refund anticipation checks (RACs), the bank opens a temporary bank account into which the IRS directly deposits the refund check. The bank waits until the IRS directly deposits the consumer's refund into the account and then issues the consumer a paper check and closes the account. The consumer picks up the check from the tax-preparer's office.

A tax preparer arranging a RAL or RAC must secure the taxpayer's written consent to disclose tax information to the lending financial institution in connection with the application. Tax preparers can deduct tax-preparation fees and additional RAL/RAC preparation fees from the customer, leaving the final RAL/RAC to be borrowed. When assisting a taxpayer in applying for a RAL or RAC, the provider may charge a flat fee for that assistance. The fee must be identical for all customers and must not relate to the amount of the refund or the financial product. If a taxpayer is approved, then a RAL is directly deposited within several business days to the taxpayer's account. If a taxpayer is approved for a RAC, then the taxpayer receives a check (either mailed or on the spot). If the RAL or RAC customer does not receive the expected tax return amount as calculated by the tax preparer, he or she is liable to the lender for additional interest and other fees, as applicable for receiving the RAL/RAC.[5] Nationally, 8 percent of people report receiving a RAL in the past five years (Applied Research and Consulting 2009).

Rent-to-Own (RTO) Agreement

The rent-to-own (RTO) industry (also known as the rental-purchase industry) consists of retailers that rent furniture, appliances, home electronics, and jewelry. RTO transactions provide immediate access to such goods for a relatively low weekly (or biweekly) or monthly payment without credit checks or a down payment. This self-renewing weekly or monthly lease for rented merchandise provides the customer with the option to purchase the good by continued payments for a specified period of time, usually 12 to 24 months, or by early payment of some specified proportion of the remaining lease payments. The customer has no obligation to continue payment beyond the current weekly or monthly period. A nationally representative survey found that 5 percent of respondents reported using an RTO store in the past five years (Applied Research and Consulting 2009).

---

[5] Internal Revenue Service, http://www.irs.gov, and Chi Chi Wu, 2004, "Building a Better Refund Anticipation Check: Options for VITA Sites," Boston: National Consumer Law Center.

Small-Dollar Loan Products and Financial Services: Literature Review Matrix

Empirical Studies of Auto Title Loans

Source	Data	Sample/Study population	Method	Findings	Access	Consumer behavior/ Substitutes	Costs	Financial literacy	Location	Policy
Applied Research and Consulting LLC. 2009. *Financial Capability in the United States: Initial Report of Research Findings from the 2009 National Survey.* New York: Applied Research and Consulting LLC.	Individual-level survey data	1,488 U.S. survey respondents of which 180 were unbanked; nationally representative	Descriptive analysis	Of all survey respondents, 7 percent reported use of an auto title loan in the last five years. Seven percent of 18–29 year-olds took out an auto title loan compared with 10 percent of 30–44 year-olds, 7 percent of 45–59 year-olds, and 4 percent of those ages 60 and over. Five percent of respondents making less than $25,000 took out an auto title loan, compared with 7 percent of those making between $25,000 to $75,000 and 10 percent of those making over $75,000. Five percent of those with less than a high school education took out an auto title loan as compared with 6 percent of those who graduated high school, 9 percent of those with some college, and 7 percent of respondents who have more than an undergraduate college degree. Of respondents considered unbanked (those without any depository account), 5 percent reported using an auto title loan while 7 percent of those considered banked used an auto title loan. Of respondents who felt they were not good at dealing with day-to-day financial matters, 7 percent used an auto title loan in the past five years, the same percentage as those who considered themselves good at dealing with day-to-day financial matters.		✓		✓		

Small-Dollar Loan Products and Financial Services: Literature Review Matrix

Empirical Studies of Auto Title Loans

Source	Data	Sample/Study population	Method	Findings	Access	Consumer behavior/ Substitutes	Costs	Financial literacy	Location	Policy
Feltner, T. 2007. *Debt Detour: The Automobile Title Lending Industry in Illinois.* Chicago, IL: Woodstock Institute and the Public Action Foundation.	Illinois court cases	61 Illinois auto title loan borrowers who were taken to court in 2005 by a licensed auto title loan company	Descriptive analysis	Nearly all the loans referenced in the Illinois court cases had terms of more than 60 days, allowing them to circumvent strong consumer protection passed by the state in 2001. Of the loans reviewed, 93 percent were structured so that the borrower made monthly, interest-only payments and a final balloon payment of the entire loan principal. These loans may contribute to a series of refinances or renewals commonly described by consumer advocates as a *cycle of debt.* Of the loans reviewed, 23 percent were used to repay a previous loan with the same lender. Overall, auto title loans were more likely to be made to male borrowers living in moderate- to middle-income communities and made against older, high-mileage vehicles. The average borrower pursued in court by a title lender faced median damages of $5,462 on a median loan of just $1,500—nearly four times the original loan principal. Included in this amount is the $268 in court and attorney fees. Borrowers often fail to appear in court, resulting in a default judgment in favor of the lender; nearly half (48 percent) of reviewed cases were granted default judgments. Eighteen percent of default auto title loans resulted in the repossession or loss of the borrower's vehicle.		✓	✓			✓
Fox, J. A., and E. Guy. 2005. *Driven into Debt: CFA Car Title Loan Store and Online Survey.* Washington, DC: Consumer Federation of America.	Individual-level data of store staff; review of online title lenders; state laws and court decisions for all 50 states	81 auto title stores in 11 states	Descriptive analysis	Over two dozen title lending bills were filed during the 2005 state legislative season. To regulate the auto title lending industry, 13 states have either enacted restrictive title loan laws or court decisions have established that title loans are regulated under pawn loan laws. Another 31 states have small loan rate cap laws or usury limits that restrain car title loan rates. Fox and Guy find that title lenders use several loan structures that evade state usury or small-loan rate caps. In some cases, lenders size their loans to fall outside rate-cap limits. In South Carolina, auto title loans are called 601 loans because the threshold for small loan rate caps is $600. In other states, auto title lenders repackage single-payment title loans as lines of credit to get around rate caps. In Virginia, Iowa, and Kansas, auto title loan companies define the industry as open-ended credit. This allows such companies to benefit from the deregulation of credit cards within those states. In other states, title lenders who make loans via the Internet export high-cost loans to consumers in protected states by using laws from states with no rate caps.		✓	✓	✓		✓

Small-Dollar Loan Products and Financial Services: Literature Review Matrix

Empirical Studies of Auto Title Loans

Source	Data	Sample/Study population	Method	Findings	Access	Consumer behavior/ Substitutes	Costs	Financial literacy	Location	Policy
				Another method used by auto title lenders is called sale-leaseback. Under sale-leaseback, the lender asserts that the borrower "sold" the car to the lender who then "leases" it back at a rate not permitted for lenders. Borrowers pay monthly fees to "lease" the item with the option to "buy" back the property at the end of the transaction. If payment is not made, the lender may repossess the property, sell it, and retain the proceeds. Fox and Guy find that only four states specifically prohibit sale-leaseback transactions.						✓
				Fox and Guy find that the median fee (which is in addition to the interest rates for loans) for customers was $18. Including the initial loan fee and the monthly finance charge, consumers would pay $63 to $181 for a $500 30-day loan term. On average, lenders loan 55 percent of the value of the vehicle. Auto title lenders charge a median 25 percent per month finance charge, which translated to 300 percent annual interest. Online title lenders quote average term rates of 24 percent to 652 percent annual percentage rate (APR).			✓	✓		
				Over 20 percent of auto title company staff were unable to provide the cost of borrowing. Staff from those companies surveyed often quoted monthly finance charges as an interest rate instead of the federally required APR. One-third of surveyed auto title lender staff quoted an annual rate as the cost of loans, while more than 6 percent refused to quote a cost rate.		✓				
Fox and Guy 2005 (cont'd)				The analysis also found that few lenders assessed the credit histories of the borrowers. Only 7 percent used Teletrack, a specialized credit reporting service, while another 7 percent performed full credit checks. Half of the lenders provided no literature on their loan products at the retail site. Twenty percent of stores posted rate information.						

Small-Dollar Loan Products and Financial Services: Literature Review Matrix
Empirical Studies of Auto Title Loans

Source	Data	Sample/Study population	Method	Findings	Access	Consumer behavior/ Substitutes	Costs	Financial literacy	Location	Policy
Tennessee Department of Financial Institutions. 2008. *The 2008 Report on the Title Pledge Industry.* Nashville, TN: Tennessee Department of Financial Institutions.	Administrative-level data	672 auto title locations representing 175 licensed auto title companies	Descriptive analysis	As of 2006, Tennessee auto title lenders are required (by the state) with the third renewal of a title pledge agreement, to make a 5 percent principal paydown reduction per month whether or not the payment is received. In the event the consumer cannot make the scheduled principal reductions, the lender may defer such payment until the end of the title pledge agreement. The Tennessee Department of Financial Institutions found that the application of a 5 percent principal reduction decreased the amount of interest and fees paid over the life of a loan by $1,045, provided that both agreements are fully satisfied at the end of the 22nd month. Seventy percent of new title loans (those agreements that were not rollovers) were for amounts under $1,000; 35 percent of all new loans were valued between $251 and $500. When assessing the income and expenses of the state's auto title lenders, bad debt (customer debt not offset by the sale of possessed vehicles) accounted for 16 percent of industry expenses. Although the industry in Tennessee was profitable, profitability was widely disparate among title providers in the state. Of 672 licensed locations, 152 reported less than $100,000 of net income or a loss.	✓		✓			✓

Small-Dollar Loan Products and Financial Services: Literature Review Matrix
Empirical Studies of Pawnshop Loans

Source	Data	Sample/Study population	Method	Findings	Access	Consumer Behavior/ Substitutes	Costs	Financial literacy	Location	Policy
Applied Research and Consulting LLC. 2009. *Financial Capability in the United States: Initial Report of Research Findings from the 2009 National Survey.* New York: Applied Research and Consulting LLC.	Individual-level survey data	1,488 U.S. survey respondents of which 180 were unbanked; nationally representative	Descriptive analysis	Of all survey respondents, 8 percent reported use of a pawnshop in the last five years. Nineteen percent of 18–29 year-olds pawned items compared with 9 percent of 30–44 year-olds, 6 percent of 45–59 year-olds, and 1 percent of those ages 60 and over. Sixteen percent of respondents making less than $25,000 used a pawnshop, compared with 7 percent of those making between $25,000 to $75,000 and 1 percent of those making over $75,000. Sixteen percent of those with less than a high school education reported using a pawnshop in the last five years, as compared with 11 percent of those who graduated high school, 7 percent with some college, and 3 percent of respondents who had more than an undergraduate college degree. Of respondents considered unbanked (those without any depository account), 26 percent reported using a pawnshop in the last five years while only 6 percent of those considered banked had used a pawnshop in the last five years. Of respondents who felt they were not good at dealing with day-to-day financial matters (e.g., checking accounts, credit and debit cards), 14 percent had used a pawnshop in the past five years while only 7 percent of those who considered themselves good at dealing with day-to-day financial matters reported use.		✓				
Caskey, J. P. 2005. "Fringe Banking and the Rise of Payday Lending." In *Credit Markets for the Poor*, edited by P. Bolton and H. Rosenthal (17–45). New York: Russell Sage Foundation.	American Business Information; InfoUSA	Pawnshops and pawnshop consumers	Descriptive analysis	The number of pawnshops nationally grew at about 6 percent or more per year through 1996. However, between 2000 and 2002, the number of pawnshops in many states declined. By 2003, the number of pawnshops, 11,683 nationally, barely exceeded the number in 1997. According to Caskey, the major reason pawn brokering lost its momentum was the rise of payday lending. Most pawnshop customers have credit profiles that prevent them from obtaining lower-cost credit from mainstream lenders. However, Caskey notes that survey data (See John Caskey, 1997, "Lower-Income Americans, Higher-Cost Financial Services," Madison, WI: Filene Research Institute) from lower-income households indicate that a majority of pawnshop customers have bank accounts, and many might be eligible for payday loans. Caskey notes that those eligible for payday loans may find several benefits in using them as compared with pawn loans. Unlike pawnshops, payday lenders are willing to make large loans, on average $250 versus $75 for pawnshops. Though payday loans carry interest rates similar to most pawn loans, the customer leaves a check with the payday lender rather than a	✓	✓				

Small-Dollar Loan Products and Financial Services: Literature Review Matrix

Empirical Studies of Pawnshop Loans

Source	Data	Sample/Study population	Method	Findings	Access	Consumer Behavior/ Substitutes	Costs	Financial literacy	Location	Policy
Caskey 2005 (cont'd)				personal possession. Caskey also speculates that consumers may simply perceive payday lenders as more respectable than pawnshops. By the late 1990s, possiblly due to consumers switching to payday loan usage, pawnbrokers expanded their consumer base. Many pawnbrokers began offering payday loans. Others began selling their goods using Internet services (e.g., Ebay). Caskey concludes that the financial services regulatory environment and trends in electronic payments, either possibly increasing payday or other alternative financial product use, are likely to be the most important factors over the next several years shaping pawnbrokering.	✓	✓				

Small-Dollar Loan Products and Financial Services: Literature Review Matrix

Empirical Studies of Pawnshop Loans

Source	Data	Sample/Study population	Method	Findings	Access	Consumer Behavior/ Substitutes	Costs	Financial literacy	Location	Policy
FDIC Unbanked/Underbanked Survey Study Group. 2009. *FDIC National Survey of Unbanked and Underbanked Households.* Washington, DC: Federal Deposit Insurance Corporation.	Unbanked/ Underbanked Supplement to the Current Population Survey	47,000 U.S. households surveyed in 2009; nationally representative	Descriptive analysis	Roughly one out of six unbanked households, those currently without a checking or savings account, have obtained funds by selling items at pawnshops in the last five years. Previously banked households were more likely to have sold items at a pawnshop than never-banked households. About one-fifth of previously banked households (21 percent) have sold items at pawnshops compared with 8 percent of never-banked households. In contrast to other alternative financial service (AFS) products, pawnshops tend to be used much less frequently. About 20 percent of unbanked households that sold items at pawnshops did so more than once or twice a year, and nearly half of unbanked households that have sold items at pawnshops almost never did so.

Approximately 16 percent of underbanked households, those that have a bank account but rely on alternative financial products, reported using pawnshops within the last five years. Compared with other underbanked households that use alternative financial products, underbanked households that pawned did so infrequently. Only 13 percent of underbanked households that use pawnshops do so at least a few times a year. This is just over one-third of the number of underbanked households who reported use of a payday loan a few times a year in the last five years. Thirty-three percent of underbanked households who pawned did so once or twice a year. Over half (55 percent) of pawnshop users pawned almost never.

Of underbanked households that used pawnshops in the last five years, 38 percent did so because they felt it was easier than qualifying for a bank loan. Thirteen percent of underbanked households turned to pawnbrokers because they could not qualify for a bank loans. Just over 20 percent of underbanked pawn users felt that pawnshops are more convenient than banks. Nearly 20 percent of underbanked households had other reasons for using pawnshops. | | ✓ | | | | |

Small-Dollar Loan Products and Financial Services: Literature Review Matrix

Empirical Studies of Pawnshop Loans

Source	Data	Sample/Study population	Method	Findings	Access	Consumer Behavior/ Substitutes	Costs	Financial literacy	Location	Policy
Fellowes, M., and M. Mabanta. 2008. *Banking on Wealth: America's New Retail Banking Infrastructure and Its Wealth-Building Potential*. Washington, DC: Brookings Institution.	FDIC Institution Directory; infoUSA; store-level data from state and federal licensing agency	Census tract locations of banks, credit unions, payday loan providers, pawnshops, and check cashers in 2007	Descriptive analysis; simulation models	There are more than 10,300 pawnshops in business. Of these locations, more than 46 percent are in low-income neighborhoods and another 30 percent are in lower-middle-income neighborhoods. The authors suggest that this finding may be an indication of pawnshops' mostly moderate- and lower-income customer base. Fellowes and Mabanta also find that about 93 percent of pawnshops are located within one mile of a bank or credit union branch, and 80 percent are located in the same neighborhood as a bank or credit union branch. This trend is only modestly different across neighborhood income groups, indicating that pawnshops are as likely to be close to branches in low-income neighborhoods as they are in higher-income neighborhoods.	✓				✓	
Johnson, R. W., and D. P. Johnson. 1998. *Pawnbroking in the U.S.: A Profile of Customers*. Washington, DC: Georgetown University, Credit Research Center.	Individual-level survey data	1,820 pawnshop customers who have borrowed within the last 12 months or who are aware of and shop at pawnshops but do not borrow money there, at 9 different pawnshops in 6 selected states	Descriptive analysis	Johnson and Johnson believe that pawnshop customers comprise an especially vulnerable population and lack sufficient alternatives for short-term loans. As reported from consumer surveys, the main reason individuals borrow from pawnshops instead of banks is that they have a much better chance of getting the loan they need. Correspondingly, Johnson and Johnson find that a high percentage of pawn borrowers who have applied for credit elsewhere have been rejected and express a desire to avoid the credit check that is part of most lending procedures. In addition, or perhaps as a result, many are uncomfortable with aspects of established financial institutions. Over 50 percent of survey respondents learned about the pawnshop from the shop sign. The most frequent pattern of pawnshop customer usage is borrowing for a few weeks or a month, redeeming the pawns then later, borrowing again and redeeming again. Household possessions are used in lieu of savings accounts and in lieu of credit checks. However, pawnshops meet only the needs for short-term blips in the household's finances. Consumers also reported that their most common alternative to pawning is to seek funds from friends or relatives. Their survey found that pawnshop customers tend to have larger households; are more likely to have had a divorce, separation, or widowhood or to have never been married; and have less education than their cohorts. The survey also found that the majority of pawnshop customers are ages 25–44. Johnson and Johnson note that this age range represents the family-raising stage of life when the demands upon a household are frequently greater than the income.	✓	✓	✓	✓		

Small-Dollar Loan Products and Financial Services: Literature Review Matrix

Empirical Studies of Pawnshop Loans

Source	Data	Sample/Study population	Method	Findings	Access	Consumer Behavior/ Substitutes	Costs	Financial literacy	Location	Policy
Johnson and Johnson 1998 (cont'd)				Also, Johnson and Johnson find that most pawnshop customers are men. Pawnshop employees suggested that even fewer women would have been active pawners if not for two factors: (1) a primary pawned item is jewelry, and (2) men are sometimes hesitant to admit that the household needs quick cash.	✓	✓	✓	✓		

Small-Dollar Loan Products and Financial Services: Literature Review Matrix

Empirical Studies of Payday Loans

Source	Data	Sample/Study population	Method	Findings	Access	Consumer Behavior/ Substitutes	Costs	Financial literacy	Location	Policy
Agarwal, S., P. M. Skiba, and J. Tobacman. 2009. "Rationality in the Consumer Credit Market: Payday Loans and Credit Cards—New Liquidity and Credit Scoring Puzzles?" *American Economic Review: Papers & Proceedings* 99(2): 412–17.	Individual-level credit card account data from a large U.S. bank and a payday loan provider	102,779 payday loan borrowers and 143,228 credit card account holders within the states where the payday lender operates; matched sample of 3,090 people	Logit regression DV (dependent variable): Credit card default	To address the question of why people borrow the authors look at individuals' liquidity over time. They find that credit card liquidity falls by $545 over the previous year on average, an amount that is much larger than the average $300 of a first-time payday borrower's loan. Additionally, the majority of liquidity deterioration happens in the five months before the payday loan is taken. These findings are contrary to the scenario in which an individual has an unexpected shock and may quickly need a small-dollar loan; in this case, one would expect to find a large plunge in liquidity near the time of payday loan use. The authors suggest impatience, general financial management, or persistent shocks as explanations for their finding average liquidity falling steadily. When analyzing the quality of information used by lenders, the authors find a substantial difference between FICO and Teletrack scores. This is most likely due to Teletrack's emphasis on information from subprime lenders (including auto title lenders and RTO establishments, in addition to payday lenders). The authors find that Teletrack scores have eight times the ability to predict payday loan default as FICO scores. The authors also conclude that credit card issuers would benefit from having frequently updated information about whether their account holders are payday borrowers. Taking out a payday loan doubles the probability of serious credit card delinquency over the next year.		✓	✓			
Applied Research and Consulting LLC. 2009. *Financial Capability in the United States: Initial Report of Research Findings from the 2009 National Survey.* New York: Applied Research and Consulting LLC.	Individual-level telephone survey	1,488 U.S. survey respondents, of whom 180 were unbanked; nationally representative	Descriptive analysis	Of all survey respondents, 5 percent reported taking out a payday loan in the last five years. Eight percent of 18–29 year-olds took out a payday loan compared with 7 percent of 30–44 year-olds, 7 percent of 45–59 year-olds, and 2 percent of those ages 60 and over. Six percent of respondents making less than $25,000 took out a payday loan, compared with 6 percent of those making between $25,000 and $75,000 and 2 percent of those making over $75,000. Eight percent of those with less than a high school education took out a payday loan, as compared with 6 percent of those who graduated high school, 6 percent of those with some college, and only 2 percent of respondents who have more than an undergraduate college degree. Of respondents considered unbanked (those without any depository account), 8 percent reported taking out a payday loan in the last five years and of those considered banked, 5 percent took out a payday loan. Of respondents who felt they were not good at dealing with day-to-day financial matters, 9 percent took out a payday loan in the past five years		✓				

Small-Dollar Loan Products and Financial Services: Literature Review Matrix

Empirical Studies of Payday Loans

Source	Data	Sample/Study population	Method	Findings	Access	Consumer Behavior/ Substitutes	Costs	Financial literacy	Location	Policy
				while 5 percent of those who considered themselves good at dealing with day-to-day financial matters took out a payday loan.						
Bertrand, M., and A. Morse. 2009. "What Do High-Interest Borrowers Do with Their Tax Rebate?" *American Economic Review: Papers & Proceedings* 99(2): 418–23.	Individual-level survey; administrative-level data	Transactions occurring March–September 2008 of 881 payday lending customers from 70 payday lending locations of a national payday lending chain	Random assignment with 3 treatment groups and 1 control group OLS regressions DV: Individual borrowed in a given pay cycle DV: Amount borrowed in any particular cycle	Disclosing how the fees accompanying a given payday loan add up over time and disclosing the typical repayment profile of payday loans result in a nontrivial reduction in the amount of payday borrowing. Individuals that take up large payday loans (as a fraction of their income) are unaffected by disclosures. The authors suggest that information disclosures might be more effective policy tools if they are combined with well thought-out regulatory limits on how much people can borrow at interest rates relative to their payback capacity.		✓	✓		✓	✓✓
Elliehausen, G., and E. C. Lawrence. 2001. *Payday Advance Credit in America: An Analysis of Customer Demand.* Washington, DC: Georgetown University, Credit Research Center.	Individual-level survey	427 customers who used a payday loan in the last year from a Community Financial Association of America	Descriptive analysis	Nearly all payday loan customers were aware of the finance charge for their most recent payday advance, but few were able to report accurate annual percentage rates despite recalling receipt of that information in truth-in-lending disclosures. According to the authors, a likely explanation is that payday loan customers used finance charges rather than annual percentage rates in decisionmaking. Most payday customers believe that people benefit from the use of credit and that payday loan companies provide a useful service. Still, the majority	✓	✓	✓	✓		✓

Small-Dollar Loan Products and Financial Services: Literature Review Matrix

Empirical Studies of Payday Loans

Source	Data	Sample/Study population	Method	Findings	Access	Consumer Behavior/ Substitutes	Costs	Financial literacy	Location	Policy
Elliehausen and Lawrence 2001 (cont'd)		company		of customers believe that payday loans are expensive, and a large percentage of customers thought the cost of payday loans was higher than fees for returned checks or late payments on debts. The small percentage of customers who were dissatisfied with their most recent new payday loan cited the high cost as the reason for their dissatisfaction. A large percentage of customers considered obtaining funds from traditional creditors, depository institutions, and finance companies. However, many payday loan customers perceived limitations in credit availability and had fewer alternatives than the population as a whole. Nearly three-fourths of payday loan customers have been turned down by a creditor or not given as much credit as they applied for in the last five years. Two-thirds of customers considered applying for credit but changed their minds because they thought they would be turned down. Payday loan customers tend to be younger and married or unmarried with children, and a relatively small percentage have low income or little education. The authors believe that the use of high-cost credit may be economically rational for a large percentage of payday loan customers. Payday loan customers were less likely than the adult population to have a bank or retail credit card. Though the quick and easy process for obtaining the payday loan was most frequently cited as the reason for choosing a payday loan, the authors believe that credit availability likely influenced the decision to borrow. About one in five payday advance customers has high consumer debt payments to income. The authors assert that payday loan credit is more likely to be a consequence than the major cause of their higher debt-payment burdens. Many payday loan customers use payday loans regularly for short periods of time. Over half of customers' longest consecutive sequences of loans were less than a month. Customers expressed disagreement with government limits on the number of times a consumer can obtain payday loans during the year.	✓	✓		✓		✓
FDIC Unbanked/ Underbanked Survey Study Group. 2009. *FDIC National Survey of Unbanked and Under-banked Households.*	Unbanked/ Underbanked Supplement to the Current Population Survey	47,000 U.S. households surveyed in 2009; nationally representative	Descriptive analysis	An estimated 6.6 percent of unbanked households, those currently without a checking or savings account, have obtained a payday loan in the last five years. Payday lending has been used by a larger proportion of unbanked households that were previously banked. This may reflect the fact that households generally need to have a bank account to get a payday loan. An estimated 11 percent of previously banked households have used payday		✓				

Small-Dollar Loan Products and Financial Services: Literature Review Matrix
Empirical Studies of Payday Loans

Source	Data	Sample/Study population	Method	Findings	Access	Consumer Behavior/ Substitutes	Costs	Financial literacy	Location	Policy
Washington, DC: Federal Deposit Insurance Corporation.				loans compared with only 2 percent of never-banked households. Among unbanked households, payday lending customers used these loans more frequently than other AFS credit customers use pawnshop or RTO agreements. Of those unbanked households that used payday lending, 33 percent used payday lending at least a few times a year. Fifty-eight percent of these households used payday lending once or twice a year.						
				Approximately 16 percent of underbanked households, those that have a bank account but rely on alternative financial products, reported using a payday loan in the last five years. Underbanked households that used payday loans use them more frequently than underbanked households that use pawnshop or RTO agreements. More than one-third (37 percent) of underbanked households that used payday lending did so at least a few times a year. Fifty-eight percent of these underbanked households used payday lending once or twice a year.		✓				
FDIC 2009 (cont'd)				Of underbanked households that used payday loan services in the last five years, 43 percent did so because they felt it was easier to qualify for than a bank loan. Sixteen percent of underbanked households turned to payday lenders because they could not qualify for a bank loan. For one-quarter of underbanked households, payday lenders were more convenient than banks.						

Small-Dollar Loan Products and Financial Services: Literature Review Matrix

Empirical Studies of Payday Loans

Source	Data	Sample/Study population	Method	Findings	Access	Consumer Behavior/ Substitutes	Costs	Financial literacy	Location	Policy
Fellowes, M. and M. Mabanta. 2008. *Banking on Wealth: America's New Retail Banking Infrastructure and Its Wealth-Building Potential*. Washington, DC: Brookings Institution.	FDIC Institution Directory; infoUSA; store-level data from state and federal licensing agencies	Census tract locations of banks, credit unions, payday loan providers, pawnshops, and check cashers in 2007	Descriptive analysis; simulation models	According to Fellowes and Mabanta's inventory of basic financial service locations, there are nearly 23,000 payday lenders in business and of those, approximately 8,000 are located in low-income neighborhoods. Ninety-five percent of all payday lenders are located within one mile of a bank or credit union branch, and 84 percent are located in the same neighborhood or census tract as a bank or credit union branch. This trend is consistent across neighborhoods of all income levels. Fellowes and Mabanta conclude that almost all payday lenders seem to be clustered around bank and credit union branches and that this is consistent with the fact that payday lender customers require their customers have a bank or credit union account to use their services. Based on these findings, Fellowes and Mabanta believe that the retail infrastructure is in place to shift moderate- and lower-income workers' demand for high-cost financial services to more affordable financial services and possibly create pathways for savings to create even more wealth over time. To measure the potential savings and investment wealth of households, the authors simulate a number of different possible demand and supply dynamics. They find that a typical payday loan customer, who pays about $600 per year for short-term payday loans, could make about $75,000 over her career if that money were instead invested in a diversified portfolio. They note that such wealth would dissipate if she regularly relied on overdraft funds as a substitute for payday loans; in most cases, payday loans are preferable to overdraft protection plans. The authors posit that most payday loan customers may instead prefer to substitute their use of payday loans with a lower-cost alternative. Looking at two alternatives (the North Carolina State Employees Credit Union and EE Savings Bond), borrowers are expected to build moderate savings, similar to if they had completely ended their payday loan consumption.	✓	✓	✓		✓	

Small-Dollar Loan Products and Financial Services: Literature Review Matrix

Empirical Studies of Payday Loans

Source	Data	Sample/Study population	Method	Findings	Access	Consumer Behavior/ Substitutes	Costs	Financial literacy	Location	Policy
Flannery, M., and K. Samolyk. 2005. *Payday Lending: Do the Costs Justify the Price?* Washington, DC: FDIC Center for Financial Research.	Adminstrative-level data	Two monoline payday lending companies operating 600 stores in 22 states	Multivariate regression DV: Store profitability	Using store data from 2002, 2003, and 2004, Flannery and Samolyk find that new payday lending stores (open for less than one year) generate negative or low profits for a few years before becoming profitable. On a per loan basis, Flannery and Samolyk find that total store operating costs—which are the cost of store operations (e.g., wages, occupancy, advertising, other) and the cost of default losses and loan-collection expenses—average $36 per loan at young stores and $25 at mature stores. However, the average total revenue of the mature stores ($349,000) exceeds that of the young stores ($253,000) by more than 38 percent. Mean store operating income (the difference between total revenue and total store operating costs) per loan is $9.8 for young stores, compared with almost $18.8 for mature stores. Flannery and Samolyk find a relatively high average cost of originating payday loans and find that default rates substantially exceed the customary credit losses at mainstream financial institutions. Therefore, a company's rate of new-store formation substantially affects its profitability. However, the location of the new-store formation has no influence on profitability. After controlling for loan volume, the authors do not find that economic and demographic conditions in the neighborhoods where stores are located have an effect on profitability, although they do slightly influence default losses. Flannery and Samolyk find no evidence that loan rollovers and repeat borrowers affect store profits beyond their proportional contribution to total loan volume. In other words, a store's loan volume is a key determinant of its profitability per se. These findings are reflective of the scant credit analysis undertaken in connection with payday loans. The authors conclude that fixed operating costs and loan loss rates do justify a large part of the high APRs charged on payday loans.			✓			

Small-Dollar Loan Products and Financial Services: Literature Review Matrix

Empirical Studies of Payday Loans

Source	Data	Sample/Study population	Method	Findings	Access	Consumer Behavior/ Substitutes	Costs	Financial literacy	Location	Policy
Prager, R. A. 2009. *Determinants of the Locations of Payday Lenders, Pawnshops, and Check-Cashing Outlets.* Washington, DC: Federal Reserve Board.	County-level data (Fellowes and Mabanta 2008); FDIC's Summary of Deposits and the Office of Thrift Supervision's Branch Office Survey; Census Bureau	Counties with bank and thrift branches, check cashers, payday lenders, and pawnshops	OLS regression DV: Payday loan stores per million capita in urban or in rural counties	Prager finds a positive significant relationship between the number of bank branches per capita and the number of payday lending stores. Conversely, an increase in limitations on the rates payday suppliers can charge is negatively associated with the number of payday lending stores per capita. The highest concentration of payday lending stores on a per capita basis are in those southern states that do not explicitly or effectively prohibit payday lending—Alabama, South Carolina, Tennessee, Mississippi, and Louisiana. Prager also finds that credit scores are a strong predictor of AFS provider concentration: counties where a larger percentage of the population has no credit score have a greater density of payday lenders, pawnshops, and check cashers, while counties where a larger percentage of the population has a subprime credit score have increased concentrations of payday lenders and pawnshops. She suggests that AFS providers may locate where the demand for their services is likely to be greatest because a significant proportion of the population does not qualify for more mainstream forms of credit.					✓	✓
Skiba, P. M., and J. Tobacman. 2008. "Do Payday Loans Cause Bankruptcy?" Working Paper.	Individual-level data; public record personal bankruptcy petitions provided online through Public Access to Court Electronic Records; personal bankruptcy filings in Texas Bankruptcy Courts	145,000 individuals whose first payday loan application is from a company's Texas outlets	Regression discontinuity DV: Personal bankruptcy filing	Skiba and Tobacman find that payday loan applicants who were approved for their first loans file for chapter 13 bankruptcy significantly more often than applicants who were rejected upon first applying. The effect of access to payday loans on bankruptcy is larger for monoline shops (where there is likely less substitution between forms of credit) than stores offering payday loans and pawn loans. To further explain, the authors demonstrate that approval for one payday loan results in a pattern of future payday loan applications: first-time applicants in the dataset who are approved apply, on average, for 5.2 more loans than rejected first-time applicants over the next 12 months. In dollar terms, this results in \$1,600 in loans and \$300 in interest payments. Skiba and Tobacman suggest that payday loan applicants have a persistent demand for credit, so, having discovered a place where credit is available, they return frequently. To determine whether households borrow on payday loans to take advantage of an upcoming bankruptcy filing, the authors compare the interest costs from payday loans and applicants' total debt interest burden at the time of bankruptcy filing and find that payday loan interest constitutes a nontrivial share of debt. The authors propose that these results are consistent with the interpretation that payday loan applicants are financially stressed; the first-time loan approval precedes significant additional high-interest-rate borrowing and the consequent interest burden	✓	✓				

Small-Dollar Loan Products and Financial Services: Literature Review Matrix

Empirical Studies of Payday Loans

Source	Data	Sample/Study population	Method	Findings	Access	Consumer Behavior/ Substitutes	Costs	Financial literacy	Location	Policy
Skiba and Tobacman 2008 (cont'd)				tips households into bankruptcy.						
				In the short-run, Skiba and Tobacman find that rejection of a first-time payday loan application increases the probability of taking out a pawn loan. However, they note that this effect dissipates quickly, and in dollar amounts, it is small compared with the observed increase in subsequent payday borrowing.	✓	✓				

Small-Dollar Loan Products and Financial Services: Literature Review Matrix

Empirical Studies of Refund Anticipation Loans and Checks (RALs and RACs)

Source	Data	Sample/Study population	Method	Findings	Access	Consumer Behavior/ Substitutes	Costs	Financial literacy	Location	Policy
Applied Research and Consulting LLC. 2009. *Financial Capability in the United States: Initial Report of Research Findings from the 2009 National Survey.* New York: Applied Research and Consulting LLC.	Individual-level survey data	1,488 U.S. survey respondents, of whom 180 were unbanked; nationally representative	Descriptive analysis	Of all respondents, 8 percent received an advance on their tax refunds using a RAL in the last five years. Twelve percent of 18–29 year-olds and 11 percent of 30–44 year-olds used a RAL compared with only 4 percent and 3 percent of those 45–59 and 65 or above. Twelve percent of respondents making less than $25,000 used a RAL compared with 7 percent of those making between $25,000 to $75,000 and 3 percent of those making over $75,000. Thirteen percent of those with less than a high school education used a RAL, compared with 9 percent of those who graduated high school, 8 percent of those with some college, and 4 percent of those with a college degree or more. More African Americans, 13 percent, used a RAL in the last five years than other racial/ethnic groups; 6 percent of Caucasians, 9 percent of Hispanics, and 5 percent of Asians reported using a RAL. Of respondents who felt they were not good at dealing with day-to-day financial matters, 11 percent used a RAL in the past five years, compared with 6 percent of those who said that they were good at dealing with day-to-day financial matters. Of unbanked respondents, 16 percent reported the use of a RAL. Only 6 percent of those considered banked used a RAL.		✓		✓		

Small-Dollar Loan Products and Financial Services: Literature Review Matrix
Empirical Studies of Refund Anticipation Loans and Checks (RALs and RACs)

Source	Data	Sample/Study population	Method	Findings	Access	Consumer Behavior/ Substitutes	Costs	Financial literacy	Location	Policy
Barr, M., and J. K. Dokko. (2008) "Third-Party Tax Adminstration: TheCase of Low- and Moderate-Income Households." *Journal of Empirical Legal Studies* 5(4): 963–81.	Detroit Area Household Financial Services survey conducted July 2005– March 2006	938 low- and moderate-income households in the Detroit metropolitan area	Descriptive analysis	Of tax-filing households, unbanked households are twice as likely to take out a RAL as banked households (60 and 30 percent respectively). Even after controlling for income and employment, these results persisted. Unbanked households make up 38 percent of RAL users, suggesting that banked households use RALs in significant numbers. The unbanked are 20 percentage points more likely than banked households to use a national chain, like H&R Block or Jackson Hewitt, when filing their taxes (60 percent compared with 40 percent). When analyzing how tax refunds were spent, the authors find few differences between RAL users and non-RAL users. Nearly 80 percent of households said they took out a RAL because they wanted to pay their bills or other debt faster. Nearly half of respondents reported the importance of taking out a RAL as a way to pay the tax preparer. Though RAL-takers cite paying down debt as a contributing reason for their RAL use, they are only 5 percentage points more likely to spend their tax refund on bills and debt compared with non-RAL takers (82 percent compared with 77 percent). Given the few differences in how RAL and non-RAL takers use their refund, Barr and Dokko feel that the recepit of a RAL is not well correlated with how individuals spend the money.		✓				
Berube, A., and T. Kornblatt. 2005. *Step in the Right Direction: Recent Declines in Refund Anticipation Loan Usage Among Low-Income Taxpayers.* Washington, DC: Brookings Institution.	IRS Stakeholder Partnerships, Education and Communica-tion Return Information Database (SPEC)	All tax filers nationally aggregated at the zip code level	Descriptive analysis	Usage of RALs declined in tax year 2002 when compared with 1999 through 2001. At their peak in tax year 2001, over 14.1 million taxpayers received RALs; this declined to 13.4 million in tax year 2002. This decline is not appreciably explained by changing incomes or the percentage of volunteer versus paid tax preparers. More than half of RAL recipients were also earned income tax credit (EITC) recipients (57 percent in 2002). In tax year 2002, 38 percent of EITC recipients obtained RALs; just 7 percent of non-EITC recipients obtained RALs. Taxpayer purchases of RALs varies widely across the country. Nearly half of all EITC recipients took out RALs in the South in tax year 2002, while less than 30 percent of EITC recipients did so in the Northeast and West. Similar variation exists across cities.	✓	✓				
Elliehausen, G. 2005. *Consumer Use of Tax Refund Anticipation*	EXCEL, a national twice-weekly	330 tax filers who took out a RAL based on their tax year	Descriptive analysis	The majority of RAL borrowers were repeat RAL users. Seventy percent of RAL customers had obtained RALs in previous years. Nearly three-fourths (72 percent) of RAL customers had three or more RALs in the past.	✓	✓		✓		✓

Small-Dollar Loan Products and Financial Services: Literature Review Matrix
Empirical Studies of Refund Anticipation Loans and Checks (RALs and RACs)

Source	Data	Sample/Study population	Method	Findings	Access	Consumer Behavior/ Substitutes	Costs	Financial literacy	Location	Policy
Loans. Washington, DC: Georgetown University, Credit Research Center.	individual-level survey conducted by International Communications Research; Survey of Consumer Finances; Survey of Consumer Attitudes	2003 refund		Consumers' primary reason for obtaining a RAL was to pay bills. Forty-one percent of RAL recipients reported they used their refund to pay bills, of which only 13 percent were from Christmas. Another 21 percent reported that their refund went toward unexpected expenditures. Fifteen percent reported not wanting to wait for their refund as the primary reason for obtaining a RAL. Virtually all RAL customers knew that their tax-preparation service offered electronic filing of tax returns. Nearly two-thirds of RAL customers discussed with the tax preparer other options for receiving their refund faster—such as electronic filing and direct deposit—before obtaining a RAL.						
				RAL customers are disproportionately from lower- or moderate-income households. Twenty-eight percent of RAL customers had incomes between $15,000 and $24,999 and 16 percent of RAL customers had incomes between $25,000 and $39,999. Nineteen percent of RAL borrowers had incomes less than $15,000. Only 26 percent of RAL users had incomes of $40,000 or more. Nearly half (47 percent) of RALs were for $3,000 or more. Small loans were not very common: just 11 percent of RALs were for less than $1,000.						
				Consumers using high-cost, short-term types of credit often have and perceive few options for borrowing. Many RAL customers borrow from other high-cost, short-term lenders. In the previous five years, 23 percent of RAL users borrowed from a pawnshop, and 18 percent borrowed from a payday loan company. Nearly half of RAL customers did not apply for credit because they thought that they would be turned down. Nearly half of EITC recipients that obtained a RAL reported being turned down or limited by a lender in the last five years—more than two times the percentage of all households experiencing turndowns or limitations and more than three times the percentage of all households perceiving limitations in credit availability.	✓	✓				
Elliehausen 2005 (cont'd)				EITC recipients were more likely than all households to have obtained a RAL: 19 percent of EITC recipients obtained a RAL, compared with 8 percent of all households. Elliehausen suggests that the higher incidence of RAL use by EITC recipients may be attributable to their disproportionate likelihood to be in the early family life cycle that is associated with high demand for credit. Thirty-six percent of EITC recipients are less than 45 years of age, are married, and have children, compared with 19 percent of	✓			✓		✓

Small-Dollar Loan Products and Financial Services: Literature Review Matrix
Empirical Studies of Refund Anticipation Loans and Checks (RALs and RACs)

Source	Data	Sample/Study population	Method	Findings	Access	Consumer Behavior/ Substitutes	Costs	Financial literacy	Location	Policy
				all households.						
				Most RAL customers lack awareness of the APR for their loans. Only about a quarter of customers recalled receiving an annual percentage rate disclosure and of those recalling receipt of an APR, 85 percent said that they did not know the rate that was disclosed. This lack of consumer knowledge suggests that RAL users are unlikely to have found APR information useful in making their decisions.						
FDIC Unbanked/ Underbanked Survey Study Group. 2009. *FDIC National Survey of Un-banked and Under-banked Households.* Washington, DC: Federal Deposit Insurance Corporation.	Unbanked/ Underbanked Supplement to the Current Population Survey	47,000 U.S. households surveyed in 2009; nationally representative	Descriptive analysis	Among unbanked households, those currently without a checking or savings account, 8 percent have used RALs within the last five years. Previously banked households are more likely to have used RALs than never-banked households. Almost 12 percent of previously banked households used RALs compared with 4 percent of never-banked households. Approximately 13 percent of underbanked households, those that have a bank account but rely on alternative financial products, reported using RALs within the last five years.		✓				
First Nations Development Institute and Center for Responsible Lending. 2008. *Borrowed Time: Use of Refund Anticipation Loans Among EITC Filers in Native American Communities.* Longmont, CO: First Nations Development Institute.	County-level data	EITC recipients in AZ, MN, MT, ND, NM, OK, OR, SD, WA, WI	OLS regression DV: RAL usage	A higher concentration of Native Americans and a greater level of urbanization were each found to be predictors of higher rates of RAL usage. Native counties are more likely to be rural, but also have higher rates of RAL usage. Many of the counties with the highest use of RALs among EITC filers using a paid preparer are very remote rural counties with reservations. Findings suggest that patterns of RAL usage in some Native communities may be different than other rural areas, and perhaps signal a targeting of this particular population by paid tax preparers offering RALs.

In nine of the ten states examined in tax year 2007, counties with Native land and and at least 10 percent of the total population identifying as Native American (Native-population communities) had higher rates of RAL usage among EITC recipients than other counties in the state. In four states (Minnesota, Montana, North Dakota, and South Dakota), RAL usage is at | ✓ | ✓ | | | | |

Small-Dollar Loan Products and Financial Services: Literature Review Matrix
Empirical Studies of Refund Anticipation Loans and Checks (RALs and RACs)

Source	Data	Sample/Study population	Method	Findings	Access	Consumer Behavior/ Substitutes	Costs	Financial literacy	Location	Policy
Masken, K., M. Mazur, J. Meikle, and R. Nord. 2008. "Do Products Offering Expedited Refunds Increase Income Tax Non-Compliance?" Paper presented at NTA Annual Conference in Taxation, Session on Issues in Taxpayer Filing and Tax Compliance.	IRS Tax Year Individual Income Tax Reporting Compliance data	Individuals who filed tax returns in 2004	Propensity scoring Linear regression DV: Misreported tax liability as a percent of income DV: Misreported tax credit amounts	least twice as high in Native-population counties. Taxpayers who used a RAL or RAC were more likely to misreport tax liability as a percent of income. Audits of RAL users resulted in a change in net tax liability 88 percent of the time compared with 76 percent for taxpayers who did not use a RAL or RAC. RAL users defaulted at higher rates than those not using a RAL or RAC (52 percent compared with 63 percent). Taxpayers using RACs had a slightly higher average change in net tax liability than those not using either a RAL or RAC (81 percent compared with 76 percent). The average age for audited taxpayers using a RAL was 33, similar to the mean age of RAC users, 34. Non-RAL and RAC taxpayers are older, averaging 43 years. Non-RAL or RAC users have significantly higher incomes than those who used one of the products. The average adjusted gross income of a non-RAL or RAC tax filer is $86,700 compared with $18,200 for RAL users and $20,000 for RAC users. In addition, RAL and RAC users are less likely to file a joint return than other taxpayers and are more likely to live in the South. Masken and coauthors report similar findings when analyzing the population of RAL and RAC users who are also EITC recipients.		✓				

Small-Dollar Loan Products and Financial Services: Literature Review Matrix
Empirical Studies of Refund Anticipation Loans and Checks (RALs and RACs)

Source	Data	Sample/Study population	Method	Findings	Access	Consumer Behavior/ Substitutes	Costs	Financial literacy	Location	Policy
Treasury Inspector General for Tax Administration. 2008. *Many Taxpayers Who Obtain Refund Anticipation Loans Could Benefit from Free Tax Preparation Services.* Washington, DC: U.S. Government Printing Office.	Individual-level survey data	350 taxpayers whose tax year 2007 accounts contained RAL indicators	Descriptive analysis	Based on survey responses, the authors conclude that if taxpayers were aware that refunds could arrive in as few as five days (this timeframe is based on a testing a new computer system), RALs might not have been as attractive to them. Eighty-five percent of the 250 respondents who confirmed receiving RALs stated that they would have been willing to wait up to nine days to receive their tax refund. Only 167 (67 percent) confirmed RAL recipients stated that their preparer explained how long it would take for the taxpayers to receive their tax refunds if they chose not to obtain the RAL. A review of IRS accounts for the 250 confirmed RAL users showed that their tax refunds were issued to lenders within 14 days. Twenty-six percent of the 250 respondents who used a RAL received debit cards from the preparers. Sixty-three percent (157 of 250) of the respondents stated that they would prefer to receive a debit card from the IRS instead of getting a RAL. Of the 250 respondents who stated that they had received a RAL, 213 (85 percent) obtained RALs because they wanted faster access to their tax refunds and 185 (74 percent) used the money to pay bills. Another 14 (6 percent) used the money to buy or repair a car or for home repairs and expenses. Eight percent stated they put the money in savings. As reported by respondents who confirmed receiving a RAL, tax return preparation and fees to obtain the RALs ranged from 5 to 25 percent of taxpayers' tax refunds. The average fee for respondents with tax refunds of less than $2,000 was $183, compared to $338 for respondents with tax refunds of more than $5,000.		✓	✓	✓		
Wu, C., and J. Fox. 2009. *Big Business, Big Bucks: Quickie Tax Loans Generate Profits for Banks and Tax Preparers While Putting Low-Income Taxpayers at Risk.* Washington, DC: Consumer Federation of America and National Consumer Law Center.	IRS Stakeholder Partnerships, Education & Communication (SPEC) Return Information Database for Tax Year 2006; company reports	Individuals who filed tax returns; RAL and RAC companies	Descriptive analysis	EITC recipients are overrepresented among the ranks of RAL consumers. Though EITC recipients made up only 17 percent of individual taxpayers in 2007, IRS data show that in 2007 nearly two-thirds (63 percent) of RAL consumers were EITC recipients, or 5.4 million families. In 2007, nearly $523 million in EITC funds were spent on RAL loan fees. EITC recipients who got RALs paid an additional $996 million in tax-preparation fees. The price of RALs has declined significantly for some of the biggest providers. In 2007, for taxpayers who received refunds, the average loan amount was about $2,700. At that loan amount, a RAL loan fee was $104 to $111. In 2009, a consumer could expect to pay from $62 to $110. The effective APR for an average RAL would be 77–140 percent. The price of		✓	✓			

Refund Anticipation Loans and Checks

Small-Dollar Loan Products and Financial Services: Literature Review Matrix
Empirical Studies of Refund Anticipation Loans and Checks (RALs and RACs)

Source	Data	Sample/Study population	Method	Findings	Access	Consumer Behavior/ Substitutes	Costs	Financial literacy	Location	Policy
Wu and Fox 2009				tax-preparation averages $183 for H&R Block and can be higher for other preparers. Altogether, the consumer might pay about $245 to $293. If the consumer chooses an independent tax preparer that charges a "document processing" or "application" fee of $40 per loan, the total loan amount could rise to as much as $285 to $333.		✓	✓			
				Independent preparers have about 70–75 percent of the paid preparer market and 40 percent of the RAL market.						
				Some individual preparers and preparer companies receive incentives when a consumer elects to receive a RAL. For example, Republic Bank & Trust advertises on its web site an incentive payment of $6 per RAL. Santa Barbara Bank & Trust pays $3 per RAL plus an additional payment of $1 to $3 depending on the loan performance of RALs. H&R Block no longer provides employees compensation per sale of RALs and RACs.						
				Several additional products have been introduced by leading RAL and RAC providers. Both H&R Block and Jackson Hewitt introduced "pay stub" and "holiday" RALs, loans made based on anticipated refunds before taxpayers received their IRS Form W-2s and could file their returns. Jackson Hewitt's version is called the ipower Line of Credit issued by MetaBank. MetaBank charges a 1.5 percent fee for the first advance from the line and a 10 percent charge per advance thereafter, plus 18 percent periodic interest. Another product that tax preparers and their bank partners offer is an "instant" same-day RAL. These instant RALs are available for an additional fee ranging from $25 to $55. Starting in 2007, H&R Block dropped RAL loan fees for those customers who received a RAL on the Block Emerald Card. The Emerald Line of Credit carries an interest rate of 36 percent plus an annual fee of $45.						

Small-Dollar Loan Products and Financial Services: Literature Review Matrix
Empirical Studies of Rent-to-Own (RTO) Agreements

Source	Data	Sample/Study population	Method	Findings	Access	Consumer Behavior/ Substitutes	Costs	Financial literacy	Location	Policy
Anderson, M. H. and S. Jaggia. 2008. "Rent-to-Own Agreements: Customer Characteristics and Contract Outcomes." *Journal of Economics and Business* 61: 51–69.	Store transaction data	7,517 RTO transaction records which originated June 2000–May 2002 from four RTO stores (of one small chain) in AL, LA, and MS	Log-normal censored regression DV: Proportion of rent paid relative to total rent if contract went to term	The authors find that 24 percent of RTO items are actually purchased, based on transactions data. This contradicts the common perception that 60–70 percent of the goods are acquired under RTO, based on customer survey data. Trying to reconcile the two yields a purchase rate of 43 percent. Anderson and Jaggia find that actual rent paid by RTO customers is far lower (median 14.7 percent of total) than the total rent customers would have paid if the contract went to term. They conclude that this reflects, in part, many customers who either return or purchase early. While some of these returns are "failed purchases," others reflect short-term need. The working poor, customers who pay under biweekly and monthly (as compared with weekly) payment schedules, and customers who pay late all pay more rent. The authors state that the data also highlight significant business risk. Unfavorable charge-offs (merchandise written off as unrecoverable) represent almost 13 percent of total charge-offs.		✓	✓			
Anderson, M. H., and R. Jackson. 2004. "Rent-to-Own Agreements: Purchases or Rentals?" *Journal of Applied Business Research* 20(1): 13–22.	Store transaction data	352,646 transaction records of RTO customers from 100 stores in 46 states 1991–2001 (95 percent of transactions originated 1998–2001)	Descriptive analysis	The paper examines the disposition of RTO agreements and concludes that they are more frequently used for short-term needs rather than as a method of acquisition. Over 51 percent of RTO agreements result in the merchandise being returned and 48 percent with the goods remaining with the customer. Interestingly, less than half of the returns (48 percent) were because the customer needed a short-term rental. The remaining returns were for collection problems (24 percent) and affordability problems (15 percent). Also of interest, most of the purchases (56 percent) came through early purchase—the customer paid a lump sum to buy before term. Early purchase is thought to be less expensive than purchasing at term. Twenty-five percent of purchases (12 percent of all agreements) were made by customers paying to term. Because only 12 percent of all agreements end with the customer paying to term, the authors conclude that APR is not the most useful information for customers. Instead, RTO contracts should provide the purchase price at different points in time. The authors reject the scenario that a significant number of RTO customers are forced to return merchandise despite making scheduled payments		✓	✓			✓

Small-Dollar Loan Products and Financial Services: Literature Review Matrix
Empirical Studies of Rent-to-Own (RTO) Agreements

Source	Data	Sample/Study population	Method	Findings	Access	Consumer Behavior/ Substitutes	Costs	Financial literacy	Location	Policy
Anderson and Jackson 2004 (cont'd)				nearly to the term of the RTO contract. They find that 90 percent of returns occur with less than 36 percent of the scheduled weekly payments made.		✓	✓			✓
Applied Research and Consulting LLC. 2009. *Financial Capability in the United States: Initial Report of Research Findings from the 2009 National Survey.* New York: Applied Research and Consulting LLC.	Individual-level survey data	1,488 U.S. survey respondents, of whom 180 were unbanked; nationally representative	Descriptive analysis	Of all respondents, 5 percent used a RTO store in the last five years. Ten percent of 18–29 year-olds used a RTO store, compared with 5 percent of 30–44 year-olds, 3 percent of those 45–59, and 0 percent of those 65 or above. Sixteen percent of respondents making less than $25,000 used a RTO store, compared with 4 percent of those making between $25,000 to $75,000 and 1 percent of those making over $75,000. Seven percent of those with less than a high school education used a rent-to-own store as compared with 6 percent of those who graduated high school, 4 percent of those with some college, and 1 percent of those with a college degree or more. More African Americans, 10 percent, used a rent-to-own store in the last five years than other racial/ethnic groups; 4 percent of Caucasians, 4 percent of Hispanics, and 1 percent of Asians reported using a rent-to-own store. Of respondents who felt they were not good at dealing with day-to-day financial matters, 7 percent used a rent-to-own store, as compared with 4 percent of those who said that they were good at dealing with day-to-day financial matters. Of unbanked respondents, 14 percent reported the use of a RTO store. Only 3 percent of those considered banked used a RTO store.		✓				
FDIC Unbanked/Underbanked Survey Study Group. 2009. *FDIC National Survey of Unbanked and Underbanked Households.* Washington, DC: Federal Deposit Insurance Corporation.	Unbanked/Underbanked Supplement to the Current Population Survey	47,000 U.S. households surveyed in 2009; nationally representative	Descriptive analysis	Nearly 12 percent of unbanked households, those currently without a checking or savings account, have used a RTO agreement in the last five years. Of the unbanked, previously banked households were more likely to have used RTO arrangements than never-banked households (18 percent compared with 7 percent). Seventeen percent of unbanked households that used RTO agreements used them at least a few times a year; nearly 40 percent used them once or twice a year. Forty-four percent of unbanked households that used RTO agreement used them almost never. Of underbanked households, those that have a bank account but rely on alternative financial products, which used RTO agreements, 44 percent used them once or twice a year and another 44 percent used them almost never. Only 12 percent of these households report using RTO agreements at least a few times a year.		✓				

Small-Dollar Loan Products and Financial Services: Literature Review Matrix

Empirical Studies of Rent-to-Own (RTO) Agreements

Source	Data	Sample/Study population	Method	Findings	Access	Consumer Behavior/ Substitutes	Costs	Financial literacy	Location	Policy
Lacko, J. M., S. M. McKernan and M. Hastak. 2000. *Survey of Rent-to-Own Customers.* Washington, DC: Federal Trade Commission. and Lacko, J.M., S. M. McKernan and M. Hastak. 2002. "Customer Experience with Rent-to-Own Transactions." *Journal of Public Policy & Marketing* 21(1): 126–38.	Individual-level survey data collected December 1998–February 1999	12,136 U.S. households of which 532 had used RTO within the last five years; nationally representative	Descriptive analysis	2.3 percent of U.S. households had used RTO transactions in the last year and 4.9 percent, in the last five years. Compared with households who had not used RTO, RTO customers were more likely to be African American, younger, less educated, have lower incomes, have children, rent their residence, live in the South, and live in nonsuburban areas. Most (67 percent) of RTO customers entered the transaction intending to purchase and most (70 percent) purchased. As a result, the authors suggest that total cost and other terms of purchase should be provided on product labels and in agreements. The authors state that APR disclosures and price restriction policies raise more difficult questions, because they could be subject to manipulation by RTO dealers, and price restrictions could limit availability. The authors state that careful analysis should be undertaken before adopting policies that would substantially limit availability of RTO transactions because most (75 percent) of RTO customers are satisfied with their experience. Nineteen percent of RTO customers were dissatisfied, with the major complaint being about high prices. Nearly half of all RTO customers had been late making a payment and 67 percent of late customers reported the treatment they received from the store when they were late was either "very good" or "good." Eleven percent of late customers reported possibly abusive collection practices. The authors concluded that these results suggest that federal regulation of industry collection practices may be unnecessary, but the most serious abuses (such as unauthorized entry into customers' homes) warrant continued attention, even if not widespread.	✓	✓				✓
McKernan, S. M., J. M. Lacko, and M. Hastak. 2003. "Empirical Evidence on the Determinants of Rent-to-Own Use and Purchase Behavior." *Economic Development Quarterly* 17(1): 33–52.	Individual-level survey data collected December 1998–February 1999	12,136 U.S. households of which 532 had used RTO within the last five years; nationally representative	Logit regression DV: RTO use DV: RTO purchase and Multinomial logit	Consumers with lower incomes (except those with incomes less than $15,000), less access to credit, less education, and that are African American are more likely to use RTO transactions with the intent to purchase. Based on these findings, the authors suggest that (1) consumers using RTO transactions to purchase are likely to be drawn from lower income levels but not necessarily the most disadvantaged groups; (2) RTO customers uses the transactions because they lack other means to obtain the merchandise, or at least obtain it as quickly; and (3) financial literacy may enable consumers to better assess the cost and make more informed	✓	✓		✓		✓

Small-Dollar Loan Products and Financial Services: Literature Review Matrix
Empirical Studies of Rent-to-Own (RTO) Agreements

Source	Data	Sample/Study population	Method	Findings	Access	Consumer Behavior/ Substitutes	Costs	Financial literacy	Location	Policy
McKernan, Lacko, and Hastak 2003 (cont'd)	State law data compiled from industry sources and court decisions		regression DV: RTO use with intent (1) to purchase, (2) to rent, (3) unsure.	decisions. State laws also are associated with RTO customers' intention of purchasing or renting from RTO stores. First, consumers living in states with total cost label disclosure laws are less likely to use RTO to purchase than are consumers living in other states, though this finding is not robust to all model specifications. The authors state that if this finding is reliable, it is consistent with a conclusion that some customers underestimate the cost in the absence of total cost disclosures and that disclosures more fully inform these consumers, leading some to make different decisions. Second, customers in states with reinstatement laws are more likely to ultimately purchase the merchandise than are customers in other states. The authors state that this preliminary finding suggests that reinstatement rights may benefit consumers by preventing the loss of merchandise if they miss payments.	✓	✓		✓		✓